D1140295

'No, I don't think Matthew's mad,' Landis said. 'He seems to have an invisible visitor.'

Chocky is Matthew's friend. He talks to her all the time. He answers her questions. And Chocky helps Matthew. She tells him things, new things, unusual things . . .

Everybody has friends. But there's something different about Chocky. Nobody can *see* her.

Is Matthew ill? Is Chocky only inside his head? Or is she a visitor . . . from another place?

John Wyndham is the pen name of John Wyndham Parkes Lucas Beynon Harris. He was born in Warwickshire, England, in 1903. When he was eight, his father left home and after that he and his mother and brother moved from place to place all over England. The family lived in hotels and John Harris went to many different schools.

After he left his last school, when he was eighteen, he tried many different jobs. He also wrote a lot of stories, but did not sell any of them. Then, in 1931, he sent a new story to an American monthly, *Wonder Stories*. *Wonder Stories* bought it, and Harris began as a writer. At this time he used the name John Beynon Harris, but he used many different names over the years. After 1939, when there was fighting in Europe, he wrote very little.

Then in 1951 he wrote a book, *The Day of the Triffids*, about the end of the world. For this book he used the name John Wyndham for the first time. *The Day of the Triffids* was soon very famous, and was a film in 1962. Many more books followed. *The Kraken Wakes* (1953), *The Chrysalids* (1955), *The Midwich Cuckoos* (1957) and *Trouble With Lichen* (1960) are also famous. *Chocky* was his last book, in 1968. He died in 1969.

The following titles are available at Levels 1, 2 and 3:

Level 1
Brown Eyes
Girl Meets Boy
The Hen and the Bull
A Job for Pedro
The Medal of Brigadier Gerard
Run for Your Life
Streets of London
Surfer!

Level 2
Baywatch
The Birds
Breakfast at Tiffany's
The Canterville Ghost and the Model
    Millionaire
The Cay
The Diary
Don't Look Behind You
Don't Look Now
Emily
Flour Babies
The Fox
Free Willy
The Ghost of Genny Castle
Grandad's Eleven
Jumanji
The Lady in the Lake
Money to Burn
Persuasion
The Railway Children
The Room in the Tower and Other
    Ghost Stories
The Secret Garden
The Sheep-Pig
Simply Suspense
Slinky Jane
Stealing the Hills
Treasure Island
The Treasure Seekers
Under the Greenwood Tree
The Wave
We Are All Guilty
The Weirdo

Level 3
Black Beauty
The Black Cat and Other Stories
Blue Beginnings
The Book of Heroic Failures
Braveheart
Calling All Monsters
A Catskill Eagle
Channel Runner
Cranford
The Darling Buds of May
Dubliners
Earthdark
Eraser
Forrest Gump
The Fugitive
Get Shorty
Goggle Eyes
Jane Eyre
King Solomon's Mines
Madame Doubtfire
The Man with Two Shadows and Other
    Ghost Stories
More Heroic Failures
Mrs Dalloway
My Fair Lady
My Family and Other Animals
Not a Penny More, Not a Penny Less
The Portrait of a Lady
Rain Man
The Reluctant Queen
The Road Ahead
Santorini
Sense and Sensibility
Sherlock Holmes and the Mystery of
    Boscombe Pool
St Agnes' Stand
StarGate
Summer of My German Soldier
The Thirty-nine Steps
Thunder Point
Time Bird
The Turn of the Screw
Twice Shy

For a complete list of the titles available in the Penguin Readers series please write to the following address for a catalogue: Penguin ELT Marketing Department, Penguin Books Ltd, 27 Wrights Lane, London W8 5TZ.

Chocky

JOHN WYNDHAM

Level 2

Retold by Robin Waterfield
Series Editor: Derek Strange

PENGUIN BOOKS

PENGUIN BOOKS

Published by the Penguin Group
Penguin Books Ltd, 27 Wrights Lane, London W8 5TZ, England
Penguin Books USA Inc., 375 Hudson Street, New York, New York 10014, USA
Penguin Books Australia Ltd, Ringwood, Victoria, Australia
Penguin Books Canada Ltd, 10 Alcorn Avenue, Toronto, Ontario, Canada M4V 3B2
Penguin Books (NZ) Ltd, 182–190 Wairau Road, Auckland 10, New Zealand

Penguin Books Ltd, Registered Offices: Harmondsworth, Middlesex, England

Copyright © 1968 by the estate of John Wyndham
First published in Great Britain by Michael Joseph Limited 1968
This adaptation published by Penguin Books 1993
5 7 9 10 8 6 4

Text copyright © Robin Waterfield 1993
Illustrations copyright © Bob Harvey (Pennant Illustrators) 1993
All rights reserved

The moral right of the adapter and of the illustrator has been asserted

Typeset by Datix International Limited, Bungay, Suffolk
Set in 12/14pt Lasercomp Bembo
Printed in England by Clays Ltd, St Ives plc

To the teacher:

In addition to all the language forms of Level One, which are used again at this level of the series, the main verb forms and tenses used at Level Two are:

- common irregular forms of past simple verbs, *going to* (for prediction and to state intention) and common phrasal verbs
- modal verbs: *will* and *won't* (to express willingness) and *must* (to express obligation or necessity).

Also used are:

- adverbs: irregular adverbs of manner, further adverbs of place and time
- prepositions: of movement, further prepositions and prepositional phrases of place and time
- adjectives: comparison of similars (*as . . . as*) and of dissimilars (*-er than, the . . . -est in/of, more* and *most . . .*)
- conjunctions: *so* (consequences), *because* (reasons), *before/after/when* (for sequencing)
- indirect speech (statements).

Specific attention is paid to vocabulary development in the Vocabulary Work exercises at the end of the book. These exercises are aimed at training students to enlarge their vocabulary systematically through intelligent reading and effective use of a dictionary.

To the student:

Dictionary Words:

- some words in this book are darker black than others. Look them up in your dictionary, or try to understand them without a dictionary first, and then look them up later.

Matthew seemed to be talking to somebody, and answering questions. But when I looked, there was only Matthew in the garden.

I first heard about Chocky when my son Matthew was twelve years old. I listened to him in the garden one day. He **seemed** to be talking to somebody, and answering questions. But when I looked, there was only Matthew in the garden. Nobody was with him.

'Mary,' I asked my wife that evening, 'does Matthew seem **odd** to you these days?'

'He talks to **invisible** people sometimes,' she said. 'Are you thinking of that, David?'

'Yes,' I answered. 'What do you think about it?'

'I think it's all right,' she answered. 'Children do that sometimes. Do you remember Piff?'

We had a daughter too, called Polly. She was eight years old then, but when she was four she had an invisible friend called Piff. When Polly went to a place, Piff went too; when Polly wanted something, Piff wanted it too. Piff was with us for some months, and then suddenly went away. We thought that Chocky was **like** Piff.

But things only got worse with Chocky. Matthew talked more and more to this invisible friend of his. 'Talked' is perhaps the wrong word. He **argued** a lot and answered many questions; he often stopped and seemed to listen to something inside his head. And he asked Mary and me a lot of very odd questions.

'Dad,' he asked me one day, 'why do people understand more things than animals? Why are animals not as clever as people, and why are some people not as clever as other people?'

'I want to sleep,' Matthew said, 'but Chocky doesn't understand. He's always asking things.'

Suddenly Matthew saw everything in the world with new eyes and asked questions about everything too. Mary and I tried to answer these difficult questions.

♦

Some days later, we heard Chocky's name for the first time. Matthew was ill, and when children are ill, they say anything. They don't think; they speak. Mary and I were in his bedroom. He moved his head about on the bed, and suddenly said, 'No, Chocky, not now. I can't understand. I want to sleep. No . . . go away! I can't tell you now. Go away, Chocky!'

Mary put her hand on his head, and Matthew opened his eyes. 'Mum,' he said, 'I'm tired. Please tell Chocky to go away. She doesn't understand.'

'Try to sleep, Matthew,' Mary said.

'I want to sleep,' Matthew answered, 'but Chocky doesn't understand. He's always asking things.'

So Mary said, 'Chocky, you must leave. Matthew's ill. Perhaps you can come back tomorrow.'

And Matthew suddenly smiled happily and went to sleep!

Down in the kitchen, Mary said, 'So Chocky is its name. Perhaps it's another Piff.'

'Perhaps it is,' I said, 'but twelve-year-olds don't usually **imagine** things like this. And it's very odd that Matthew sometimes calls Chocky "him" and sometimes "her", too.'

'But it's all right,' Mary said. 'Piff only stayed for a short time. I don't think Chocky's going to be with us for long.'

After this, Matthew talked more easily to us about

Matthew asked some very odd questions for a twelve-year-old: How long is an hour?

Chocky, because he knew that we now knew his – or her – name.

'How can we talk about Chocky?' I said. 'Is Chocky a boy or a girl? A "he" or a "she"?'

'She doesn't know,' Matthew said. 'I asked, but he doesn't seem to understand the question.'

'It's something people usually do know quite well,' I said.

Matthew said that Chocky was like a boy *and* like a girl, but seemed to be a girl more than a boy.

'Let's call Chocky "her", then,' I said, and Matthew said that was all right.

◆

Mary argued that Chocky was not **real**, and that when we talked to Matthew, we were wrong to make Chocky seem real for him. 'Matthew only imagines Chocky,' she said, 'but soon he's going to get a picture in his **mind**, and then it's going to be more difficult for Chocky to go away.'

But there was something very real about Chocky. She seemed to come from outside Matthew, not from inside him. 'I don't think that Matthew is only imagining Chocky,' I told Mary.

The questions Matthew asked me were very odd questions for a twelve-year-old to ask. Why are there seven days in a week, not eight? Where is the world? How long is an hour? Children aren't usually interested in these questions: an hour is an hour for them, that's all; and they don't think that there are other places, only the world.

Soon Chocky was real for Polly too. Before Chocky

*One evening, Mr Trimble, a teacher from Matthew's school,
visited us.*

arrived, Polly and Matthew played a lot of games together. But now Polly saw that Matthew had more time for Chocky than for her, and this made her sad. The two children argued all the time.

One evening, Mr Trimble, a **teacher** from Matthew's school, visited us. I gave him a cup of coffee and waited for him to speak.

'Are you good at **arithmetic**, Mr Gore?' he asked me.

'No,' I answered.

'So you are, then, Mrs Gore,' he said to Mary.

'No, not me,' Mary said, 'I don't understand arithmetic.'

'That's odd,' Mr Trimble said, 'very odd. You see, Matthew is asking some interesting questions in school these days.'

So Chocky was not only in our home. She went to school with Matthew, too.

'Matthew is not a bad student,' Mr Trimble said, 'but he doesn't ask many questions usually – and now these are not easy questions. He seems to want all arithmetic to be different. He says our usual ten numbers are too difficult. He wants the only numbers to be "yes" and "no" – "yes" for "on", and "no" for "off". We call it "Binary Arithmetic".'

The next day, I asked Matthew about this arithmetic. I wrote on some paper:

YNYYNNYY

'What number is that, Matthew?' I asked.

He looked at it quickly and said, '179.'

'Do you think this arithmetic is easier than our usual arithmetic?'

'Chocky does,' he answered. 'Chocky showed it to me. You start with 1 on the right, the next place to the left is 2, the next is 4, the next is 8 . . . And when a place has "yes", that number is in; when a place has "no", that number is out. So your number is: 1 – yes, 2 – yes, 4 – no, 8 – no, 16 – yes, 32 – yes, 64 – no, 128 – yes. And that makes 179.'

I said I understood.

'Chocky thinks we're **silly** to have ten numbers, when you can work with only two things – yes and no,' said Matthew.

'Which book was this arithmetic in?' I asked.

'I *told* you, Dad,' Matthew said. 'It *wasn't* in a book, Chocky and I talked about it.'

Then he stopped and thought for a minute. 'Dad,' he asked, 'do you think I'm **mad**?'

'No,' I said quickly. 'Why do you think that?'

'Because when people hear things inside their head, other people say they're mad,' Matthew said.

'I don't understand everything about Chocky,' I said, 'but I do know that he, she or it is not making you mad. You're only interested in different things, that's all. And that's good, not bad.'

◆

But a week later, Mary and I began to be more afraid. I bought a new car, and Matthew was very excited when I brought it home. He came out of the house and looked at the car with a smile on his face. Then he suddenly stopped smiling and seemed to listen to something inside his head, so I knew Chocky was there. Then Matthew went more and more red in the face, got more and more

14

Suddenly Matthew started to cry, and he ran back into the house and up to his room.

*Matthew came back late in the afternoon — and a policeman
was with him.*

angry. Suddenly he started to cry, and he ran back into the house and up to his room. I went to see him.

'Why are you crying?' I asked.

'I showed the car to Chocky,' he said, 'and she said it was silly.'

'Why is it silly? It's a nice car.'

'*I* don't think it's silly, Dad,' Matthew said. 'I argued with Chocky and said that the car was beautiful; but she said it makes a lot of dirty smoke, and isn't quiet, and can't go fast, and is silly. Sometimes I'm tired of Chocky, Dad.'

Mary was quite afraid for Matthew. He was very, very angry. 'Please listen to me, David,' she said. 'Matthew must see a doctor.'

I remembered an old friend called Roy Landis; he was a **psychiatrist**. I spoke to him on the telephone and told him about Chocky and Matthew. Landis said he wanted to come and see Matthew.

When I told Matthew, he was happy, because somebody outside the family was interested in Chocky. He was always careful and never talked about Chocky in school. 'I don't want people to think I'm mad,' he said. 'But I like to talk to other people about Chocky.'

The day before Landis's visit, we all went in the new car to the sea. After lunch, Matthew walked away from us into the village. He came back very late in the afternoon – and a policeman was with him.

'Somebody found this young man on his boat,' the policeman said, smiling quietly behind Matthew's back. 'He was angry about it and he called the police. But because the boy's only young, we brought him back here to you. And here he is.' Matthew must never go on other people's boats again without asking, the policeman told us.

Matthew said he was sorry, and the policeman went away. Then Matthew said, 'I only looked in the boat.'

'You were lucky,' Mary said. 'The policeman was nice and friendly.'

'Yes,' Matthew said. 'But I wanted to show Chocky some boats and ships.'

'So Chocky was with you again?' I asked.

'Yes,' Matthew said.

Polly stopped her game and went quiet.

'Chocky must think ships are silly too,' I said.

'Yes, she does,' Matthew said. 'She says they're too slow. She says when people learn to fly with their minds, that's going to be better, cleaner and faster.'

'I don't quite understand,' I said. 'Where does Chocky come from?'

'I asked her that,' Matthew said, 'but she can't tell me.'

'Why not?' Mary asked.

'Because. . .' Matthew began, but then stopped. 'Because it's difficult to understand. You see, where are you, Dad?'

'I'm next to you, and near the sea, and two yards away from the car, and . . .'

'See, Dad? You can say, "I'm near this and next to that." But when you *can't* say something like that, you can't answer the question. You can't say where you are. And Chocky can't say where she is, because she doesn't know.'

◆

Landis came for lunch the next day. After lunch, he and Matthew went to Matthew's bedroom; they only came out four hours later.

Mary and I put the children to bed and then sat down with Landis.

'Does Matthew imagine a lot of things, David?' he asked me.

'No more than other children,' I said.

'I think Matthew is very interesting,' he said. 'In the old days, people thought invisible visitors sometimes came into other people's minds and lived there. But that was wrong, so . . .'

'So what must we think?' I asked. 'Is Matthew mad?'

'No, I don't think he's mad,' Landis said. 'He *seems* to have an invisible visitor. You know that Matthew always speaks in his language and with his words, not Chocky's.'

'Yes,' we said.

'Matthew says he can't easily tell us these things, because he doesn't know the English words. But when you or I learn about something from a book, we understand the book's words, so we can tell other people about it with the book's words. Right? And when you imagine things, you are the maker of those things, so you understand them and can easily tell other people about them. So why is it difficult for Matthew to tell us? Why hasn't he got the words? And what about that arithmetic? When you read about it in a book, you don't see "yes" and "no" or "Y" and "N", you see 0 and 1. And Matthew says that it doesn't come from a book. I think he's right – it doesn't.'

Mary started to get angry. 'You're not helping,' she said, 'when you say that Chocky is a visitor from outside Matthew's mind, because you are saying at the same time that visitors like that aren't real, and that this is all a big mistake. What *can* we think?'

19

'I don't know, Mary,' Landis said. 'What can I do? Matthew says that Chocky moves with her mind because it's easy and fast. She thinks she's in a place, and then she *is* in that place. What do you think about that? What book has that in it?'

'A book at school, perhaps,' Mary said.

'I don't think so,' Landis said. 'And no book for twelve-year-olds says things like that. And Matthew says that Chocky's time is not the same as our time, too; she comes from a different place and lives in a different time. And Matthew *argues* with Chocky.'

'Now *you* seem to think that Chocky is real,' Mary said angrily.

'Yes, because she *does* seem to be real. You told me about Piff, but Chocky is not like Piff,' Landis said.

'Then what is she?' Mary asked.

'I'm afraid I don't quite know,' Landis said.

Mary turned to me. 'You see, David,' she said. 'He's not helping. I don't think he's right. Matthew imagines Chocky; she's not real. Matthew only reads too many books, and then imagines things. And Mr Landis says that he doesn't understand Chocky; so he must be wrong.'

I stayed quiet. Landis and Mary argued for half an hour, and then Landis left.

◆

Near the beginning of the school's summer holidays, I came home from the office one day, and Mary showed me some pictures. 'I found these in Matthew's room,' she said.

The pictures were very exciting. They showed the

'Now you *seem to think Chocky's real,' Mary* said
angrily.

usual things – people, animals, buildings – but all these things were different. The people in the pictures were long and thin. 'Anybody can see that these are people,' I said, 'and that these are dogs. But who sees people and dogs like that? Only different eyes can see people like that.'

The pictures were very, very good. The lines and colours were strong; the people seemed to live. They were not like Matthew's usual pictures.

I called Matthew and showed him the pictures. 'Did *you* **paint** these pictures, Matthew?' I asked, smiling.

'Yes,' he said slowly. 'Well . . . my hands painted them.'

'I don't understand,' I said.

'Chocky helped, you see,' Matthew said.

'How?' Mary asked.

'I was at school,' Matthew said. 'I was angry because I can't paint, and the teacher, Miss Soames, told me my other pictures were no good. I knew she was right. Then Chocky said that I must not think that pictures are like photographs. I must look at things differently, she said. I tried, but the pictures were all wrong again.'

Matthew stopped for a minute. 'What happened next?' I asked.

'Chocky said she wanted to try to paint. "Be quiet," she said, "and turn off your mind." But when you *try* to think of nothing, it's very difficult, you know. At last it got easier and then Chocky painted the pictures with my hands.'

'Does Chocky see people long and thin?' I asked.

'Yes, she does,' Matthew said. 'And I learned quickly. Now I can turn my mind off and think of nothing when I want to, so Chocky can do things through me.'

'Anybody can see that these are people, and that these are dogs. But who sees people and dogs like that?'

'What happens when Chocky does that?' Mary asked.

'Well, when I try to ride a bike with no hands, it's nearly the same,' Matthew said. 'But Chocky is driving me, so it isn't dangerous . . . I know it's difficult to understand.'

'Do you think that it's good for Chocky to drive you?' Mary asked. 'You're Matthew, not Chocky.'

'I know, Mum,' Matthew said, 'but *I* painted the pictures too. Miss Soames said the pictures were very good, but she looked at me very oddly when she saw them. "Usually, you can't paint, Matthew," she said to me. "Paint a picture in front of me." So I did, and when I finished, she took the picture away with her.'

Soon Matthew went up to bed. When he left the room, Mary began to cry. 'David,' she said, 'what's happening? I'm afraid for him.'

'Don't be afraid,' I said. 'He's all right.'

'But this Chocky is nearly stronger than my Matthew now,' Mary said. 'She "drives" him, he said.'

♦

For our holiday that summer, we went to North Wales and took a small house by the sea in Bontgoch with some friends called Alan and Phyllis Froome. Alan and Phyllis had two children too. All the first week, the four children played happily together on the beach.

'But don't play near the river,' Alan told the children.

'Why not?' Polly asked.

'Because when the river arrives at the sea,' I said, 'it's very strong, and it can carry you away, far out to sea, in a minute or two.'

On the Monday of the second week, Mary and I left

our children with the Froomes and went out in the car for the day. We had a good time: we walked and climbed in the mountains, and ate lunch outside, under the warm sun and a blue sky. We arrived back in Bontgoch in the evening, tired and happy.

But when we went into the house, we looked at Alan's and Phyllis's faces and knew something was wrong.

'Was there an accident?' Mary asked Phyllis.

'Yes, but everything is all right now,' Phyllis said. 'The children are sleeping in their beds. They fell in the river.'

Mary and Phyllis went up to see the children.

'What happened?' I asked Alan. He sat there, white-faced, with a drink in one hand.

'They're all right now,' he said, 'but they were in a lot of danger.'

'Yes, but what happened?' I asked him again.

'All four children were out on that old **jetty**,' he said, 'when a boat up the river broke away and hit the jetty hard. The old jetty broke. Our two children jumped away, but Polly and Matthew went into the water.'

He stopped and had a drink. I waited to hear more.

'Colonel Summers saw everything. "They're going to die," was his first thought. You know that the river is very strong there. But then Matthew swam over to Polly and helped her. Mr Evans saw it too. Colonel Summers quickly got his boat and went after the two children. By the time he got to them, they were over a mile out to sea. But Matthew helped Polly all the time. They climbed into the boat and the Colonel brought them back to the beach. He says he never saw anything more **brave**.'

We looked at Alan's and Phyllis's faces and knew something was wrong.

Now I wanted a drink too. Alan brought me one. 'Yesterday, I watched Matthew in the sea,' he said. 'David, he can't swim.'

'I know,' I said quietly.

I went up to the children. 'Polly's sleeping,' Mary said.

I went into Matthew's room. He was in bed with his eyes open.

'How are you, Matthew?' I asked.

'OK,' he said. 'We were very cold, but we had a hot bath when we came in.'

'Everybody's saying that you were very brave,' I said.

'No, I wasn't, Dad,' he said.

'Yes, you were,' I said. 'But I know that you can't swim.'

'No, I can't,' he said. 'But . . . Chocky can . . .'

'How did it happen?' I said.

'I saw the boat suddenly hit the jetty,' he said, 'and then we were in the water. I was afraid. Polly was nearly under the water. I tried to swim, but I was no good at it. Then I heard Chocky. She seemed angry with me. I turned off my mind again. And . . . I swam. I tried to learn to swim from you and from my teachers, but swimming was too difficult; but then Chocky suddenly made it easy. So, you see, Dad, I'm not brave: I was afraid. Chocky helped Polly, not me.'

◆

Two days later, the story about the brave boy swimmer was in all the **newspapers** in North Wales. And two weeks later, after the holidays, when we were back at home, the television had the story. Matthew was famous.

The newspaper and TV people arrived at our front door.
They all wanted to talk to Matthew.

The newspaper and TV people arrived at our front door. They all wanted to talk to Matthew.

'Don't talk to the newspaper or television people any more,' I told him. I was afraid. These newspaper people are clever. Matthew nearly told one of them about Chocky, and they were very interested. First he was not a swimmer, and then suddenly, when he and his sister were in danger, he swam. This made a good story for the newspapers.

But we were unlucky: Miss Soames, not Matthew, made things worse. She showed one of Matthew's new pictures to some people in London. The newspaper people soon heard about this picture, and now they had two stories: the brave boy swimmer was a very good painter too.

'I don't like that psychiatrist, Landis,' Mary said, 'but Matthew must see somebody. Every day and every night, the newspaper and TV people are trying to talk to us. All this must stop. I want things to be the same as they were before; I want *Matthew* to be the same as he was before.'

I met Landis, and he told me about Sir William Thorbe. He was one of the most famous doctors in the country; everybody said that he understood people's minds.

I spoke to Sir William on the phone. 'Yes, Mr Gore,' he said. 'I read the newspapers, so I know about your son. He seems very interesting. How can he suddenly paint these good pictures? And how can he suddenly swim like that? Can you bring Matthew to see me next week, on Wednesday?'

We went to the beach again that weekend. Matthew

'Chocky looked at them angrily through my eyes,' Matthew
said. 'They all ran away.'

painted some more pictures – they were better than the earlier ones. 'Chocky is learning to see through my eyes better, you see,' he said.

On Tuesday, Matthew came home from school with a black eye. A bigger boy hit him, because he thought Matthew was too famous.

'But suddenly all the other boys ran away,' Matthew said.

'Why did they run away?' I asked.

'Chocky got angry,' he said. 'I stood up and Chocky looked at them angrily through my eyes. They all ran away.'

On Wednesday, I left my office early and met Matthew at the train station. We went together to Sir William Thorbe's office in London. When I went back to Sir William's office two hours later, I asked him, 'What do you think?'

But Sir William only said, 'I'm going to write to you. Please wait for my letter.'

'What happened?' I asked Matthew when we were in the train.

'He asked me some questions,' Matthew said. 'Then he said he wanted me to sleep. I watched things go round and round, and then I don't remember what happened after that.'

♦

That weekend, on the Sunday, Matthew went out on his bike and painted some more pictures. He seemed sad. When he came home in the evening, he went quietly up to his room. Mary followed him and tried to give him some food, but he told her that he wasn't hungry. I went up to his room.

'What's wrong, Matthew?' I asked.

He said nothing, but showed me some more pictures. Most of them were pictures of things he saw when he was out on his bike. They were as good as usual. But one picture was different. It was not a picture of any place in our world. This place was big and flat, with some small round things near the front and mountains far away. The mountains were the only interesting things in the place. Everything was red and brown; only the blue sky was light-coloured. The place seemed to be very hot.

I wanted to ask Matthew about this place, but he started to cry. 'Dad,' he said, 'these are the last pictures. Chocky's going away.'

I left him. Later, when I told Mary that Chocky was going away, she was happy. She smiled for the first time in weeks.

'Do you see?' she said. 'I was right. Chocky is another Piff. I think Sir William told him the other day, "You must say goodbye to Chocky. You're going to be sad, but she must go." And Chocky *is* going away, quite soon after Matthew met Sir William.'

'Perhaps you're right,' I said. 'But . . .' I started to tell Mary about the odd picture, but then I stopped. She was happy now.

The next day, I asked Matthew about the picture.

'Chocky lives there,' he said. 'It's not a nice place. She often said that our world is beautiful, but that we're making it dirty with our factories and cars and everything.'

'What are those round things in the front of the picture?' I asked.

This place was big and flat, with some small round things near the front and mountains far away.

'I don't quite know,' Matthew said. 'Sometimes Chocky seemed to say that they're buildings, and sometimes that they're towns.'

'Don't tell Mum about this painting, please, Matthew,' I said.

'No,' Matthew said, and then he was quiet.

'Is Chocky here?' I asked.

'No, Dad,' Matthew said. 'Chocky is never going to be here again.' He started to cry. 'I had Chocky inside me, so when she went it was much worse than when a friend goes away. A friend isn't inside you . . .'

On Monday, Matthew was sad, but he went to school. Sir William's letter arrived that day. It was short and showed little understanding, I thought.

Matthew was afraid to swim before, Sir William said, but was more afraid about Polly when he saw her in danger, so he helped her. And Matthew always wanted to paint, but never painted before perhaps because, when he was very young, somebody told him he was a bad painter. Matthew only imagined this thing called 'Chocky', he said, but because she was real for him, 'Chocky' helped Matthew to do things. But Chocky was only inside Matthew's mind.

I was not happy with the letter. It left out important questions; it made things too easy. I knew that Chocky was different. Why was his letter silly, when Sir William was the most famous psychiatrist in the country?

♦

What is the right thing to do when somebody **kidnaps** your son? On Friday, I worked late in the office, but Mary phoned me. 'Matthew is not home from school,' she said. 'He's two hours late. I phoned the school, but they said he left at the right time. David, I'm afraid.'

I took the first train home. We phoned the hospitals and the police. Matthew was not in any hospital; the police sent somebody to talk to us. The newspaper people came to our house again.

We waited all weekend. There was nothing. On Sunday, the father of a school friend of Matthew's telephoned.

'Is that Mr Gore?' he said. 'My boy Lawrence says he saw Matthew in a car outside the school on Friday. He didn't tell me before. Then we read the story in the newspapers.'

'Thank you,' I said. 'I'm going to tell the police now.'

'Good. I hope they find your son quickly,' he said.

So we knew that this was a kidnapping. But why does anybody kidnap a child? Because he wants money, usually. But we weren't rich. We waited, and waited, and waited . . . Those were the worst ten days in our family. Nobody said anything; everybody was quiet. Mary seemed ill; Polly wasn't interested in her games. We all began to think that Matthew was dead.

Then, 200 miles away in Birmingham, a boy walked up to a policeman in the street early one morning.

'Can I help?' the policeman asked.

'I want to go home,' the boy said.

'Where do you live?'

'In Hindmere.'

'And what's your name, young man?' the policeman asked.

'Matthew Gore,' Matthew said.

35

Matthew told his story to the police two or three times, and saw a doctor. Then he talked to Mary and me.

'I started home from school,' he said. 'A man stopped his car in front of me. He got out of the car and asked me, "Do you know Densham Road? I'm trying to find Mr Gore." "That's my father," I said. "Get in the car, then," he said. "You can show me your house." He seemed nice. After I got in the car, I don't remember anything. Then I was in a hospital.'

'A hospital?' Mary asked.

'Yes,' Matthew said. 'Everybody wore white coats. They said that I broke my leg in a car accident. They were very nice, but I wanted to see you and you didn't come. Where were you?'

'Nobody knew you were there,' I said. 'Those people in white coats kidnapped you. What happened in the hospital?'

'I read a lot of books,' Matthew answered. 'There was no TV or radio. They gave me a lot of **injections**.' He showed us his arm. 'I wrote you two letters.'

'We never got any letters from you,' Mary said.

I phoned the doctor and asked him about the injections. He said that they weren't dangerous. Matthew told Mary more about the 'hospital' and the people there.

'After about a week, they said my leg was better,' he said. 'Then they gave me one last injection. In the night, they drove me to Birmingham, and in the morning I found a policeman, and . . . here I am. Did you pay a lot of money to the kidnappers, Dad?'

'After I got in the car, I don't remember anything. Then I was in a hospital.'

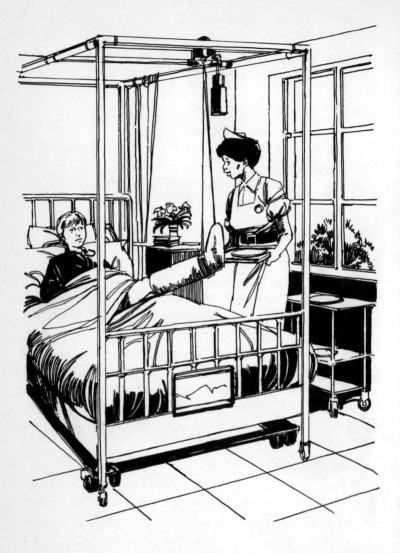

'They said that I broke my leg in a car accident. They were
very nice, but I wanted to see you.'

'No,' I said. 'Nobody asked us for any money.'

'Then it *wasn't* a kidnapping,' Matthew said. 'Kidnappers always ask for money.'

He was tired, so he went to bed. Then at last Mary started to cry. She cried and cried in my arms.

♦

Matthew stayed at home all the next week. At midnight on Friday, he came to see me.

'Is Mum in bed?' he asked.

'Yes,' I said. 'Why do you want to know?'

'I want to talk to you,' he said. 'Or Chocky wants to talk to you.'

'Is Chocky back?' I asked.

'Yes, she is,' Matthew said, 'but only for a short time. She wants to tell you some things. She doesn't want *me* to tell you these things: she wants me to turn off my mind again, and then *she* can talk to you.'

He sat in a chair. First he opened his mouth two or three times, with no sound. Then he said, 'This is Chocky. I want to talk to you, because I'm never coming back again after this. Matthew's mother is happier now, but I was never dangerous for Matthew. Do you know that?'

'Yes, I do,' I said. 'But who, or what, are you?'

'I'm an **explorer**,' Chocky said. 'I come from far away. My world sends explorers like me everywhere. We explore other worlds. We move with our minds, and stay in other people's minds. We can't stay in everybody's minds. Most older people's minds are closed, but Matthew's is not. His mind is young and open. I must talk to you through

39

Matthew because I can't live in your mind, you see.'

'Why do you explore other worlds?' I asked.

'Our world is too small for all of us,' she said, 'so we must find other worlds. When we find a good world, many of us are going to go and live in it.'

'Is our world good for you?' I asked.

'No,' Chocky said. 'It's very beautiful, but it is too cold and wet. I only stayed here because explorers are teachers too. Most worlds have no living animals; some worlds have living people, but they can't learn. Only some people can understand difficult things. When we find people like that, we teach them. We help them to learn and to make their world better. But I can't teach Matthew.'

'But he's clever,' I said.

'Yes,' Chocky said, 'he's clever, but I made mistakes, so I must leave before I can teach him. I'm young too, you see, and I wasn't an explorer before.'

'What were your mistakes?' I asked.

'Explorers can't *like* people,' Chocky answered. 'They can only look at people. But when I saw that Matthew wanted to paint, I helped him to paint; and when Polly and Matthew were in the water, I helped Matthew to swim.'

'I am very, very happy about that,' I said.

'But nobody must know that an explorer is there,' Chocky said. 'You soon knew. You knew that I was real, something from outside Matthew's mind. And Landis nearly knew too. But Sir William Thorbe was the worst.'

'Tell me about that,' I said. 'What happened with Sir William?'

'He quickly knew that I was real,' Chocky said, 'and that I came from another world. I saw that he was very excited. Then I understood my mistake.'

'Why?'

'Thorbe told other people,' Chocky said. 'They're not bad people, but they have their work. And they think that their work is more important than one small boy and his family. They know that I can move by my mind. They want to learn this too: then they can sell it for millions of pounds. So they kidnapped Matthew. They gave him injections, and he talked. He told them everything. Luckily, Matthew can't help them, because I taught him nothing important. They only learned that I was real, but they learned nothing more important than that. So they sent him home. Now they're always watching him; they're waiting for me to come back. But I'm never going to come back, because these people are dangerous to Matthew. So now I must say goodbye.'

'Are you going back to your world?' I asked.

'No,' she said. 'I must finish my work in your world. I'm going to stay here, but not inside Matthew. I must be careful. I'm going to give different lessons to different people. One day, perhaps, because of my teaching, your people are going to understand.'

'Before you go, Chocky,' I said, 'what are you? Can Matthew paint you for me?'

'No,' Chocky said, 'he can't do that. I'm very, very different from you. Now please go. I want to say goodbye to Matthew.'

'All right,' I said. 'Goodbye, Chocky.' And I left the room, quite sadly.

They gave Matthew injections, and he talked. But they learned nothing important.

All this happened a long time ago. Matthew was young, so he wasn't sad for very many days. He is a well-known painter now. We sometimes remember Chocky, and talk about her, but not when Mary or Polly are there. 'And where in the world is Chocky now?' I often think. Who knows?

EXERCISES

Vocabulary Work

Look back at the 'Dictionary Words' in this story. Do you know the meaning of all the words?

1 Look at these words:

odd	kidnap	silly	psychiatrist
invisible	real	explorer	argue
mad	teacher	brave	

Find: six *adjectives*, three *nouns* (for people) and two *verbs*. Write a sentence to show the meaning of each one clearly.

2 Find words to match these definitions.

a something students learn at school

b something you can read

c something a doctor gives you

d something you can do to make a picture

3 Write three sentences with the words in these groups, to show their meanings clearly.

a seem/like (adverb)   c boat/jetty

b imagine/mind (noun)

Comprehension

Pages 7–18

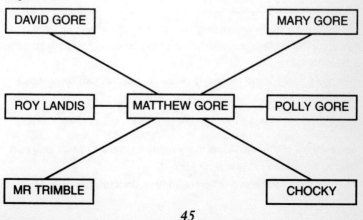

1 Look at the names of the people above. Matthew knows these people. Write who the people are, e.g. *David Gore is his father*.

2 Are these sentences true (√) or not true (×)?

a Matthew was ten years old.

b Polly had an invisible friend called Piff.

c Chocky liked Mr Gore's new car.

Pages 19–31

3 Answer these questions.

a What does Matthew 'turn off' so that Chocky can do things through him?

b Where did the Gores go for their holiday?

c Why did the old jetty break?

d Who told the newspaper people about Matthew's picture?

e Why did a bigger boy hit Matthew at school?

Pages 32–43

4 Who said these things? Who to?

a 'A man stopped his car in front of me.'

b 'Nobody knew you were there. Those people in white coats kidnapped you.'

c 'We never got any letters from you.'

d 'I am an explorer.'

5 Chocky taught Matthew to do many different things. Name *three* of the things.

6 Write two or three sentences about why some people kidnapped Matthew. (Who were they? Where did they take him? What did they do to him? Why?)

7 Why did Chocky leave Matthew? (Answer in one or two sentences.)

Discussion

1 Do you think the things in this story really happened? Why? Why not?

2 Do you *like* Chocky? Why? Why not?

3 Think of this story with a different ending: Chocky stays with Matthew

and doesn't leave him. Is Matthew going to live happily? Or is he going to be in more danger?

Writing

1 Look at the picture on page 30. Now write three sentences about Matthew's face, body and clothes.
2 You are one of the newspaper reporters. Write your story about Matthew the brave boy swimmer, and about his pictures (in about 200 words).
3 Dangerous things happen to Matthew in this story. Write about a time when *you* were in danger (in about 150 words).